Keto Vegetarian Diet Cookbook

Ketogenic Plant-Based Diet for a Healthy and Balanced Lifestyle

Lauren Bellisario

by reading this document, the reader agrees that under no circumstances is the author responsible for any losses, direct or indirect, which are incurred as a result of the use of information contained within this document, including, but not limited to, — errors, omissions, or inaccuracies.

Table of Contents

Breakfast Naan Bread

Preparation time: 5 minutes
Cooking time: 20 minutes
Serving: 6

Nutritional Values (Per Serving):
- Calories:263,
- Total Fat:25.2 g,
- Saturated Fat: 6.4g,
- Total Carbs:3 g,
- Dietary Fiber: 1g,
- Sugar:2 g,
- Protein:7 g,
- Sodium: 376mg

Ingredients:
- ¾ cup almond flour
- 1 tsp salt + extra for sprinkling
- ½ tsp baking powder
- 2 tbsp psyllium husk powder ⅓ cup olive oil
- 2 cups boiling water Butter, for frying

Directions:
1. In a bowl, mix the almond flour, ½ teaspoon of salt, baking powder, and psyllium husk powder.

2. Mix in some olive oil and boiling water until thick batter forms. Stir thoroughly and allow the dough rising for 5 minutes.
3. Divide the dough into 6 to 8 pieces and mold into balls. Place the balls on a parchment paper and flatten with your hands.
4. After, melt the butter in a frying pan and fry the naan on both sides until golden color.
5. Transfer the naan to a plate and use warm for breakfast.

Blueberry Soufflé

Preparation time: 15 minutes
Cooking time: 20 minutes
Serving: 4

Nutritional Values (Per Serving):

- Calories:478
- Total Fat: 46.8g
- Saturated Fat:27.3 g
- Total Carbs: 8 g
- Dietary Fiber: 4g
- Sugar: 1g
- Protein: 11g
- Sodium: 257mg

Ingredients:
For the blueberry sauce:

- 1 cup frozen blueberries
- 2 tsp erythritol
- 1 tbsp water

For the omelet:

- 4 egg yolks, room temperature
- 3 tbsp erythritol, divided
- 3 egg whites, room temperature
- 1 tsp olive oil
- ½ lemon, zested to garnish

Directions:

For the blueberry sauce:

1. Pour the blueberries, erythritol and water in a small saucepan over medium heat. Cook with occasional stirring until the berries soften and become syrupy, 8 to 10 minutes. Stir in the vanilla, turn the heat off, and set aside to cool slightly.

For the omelet:

1. Preheat the oven to 350 F.
2. In a large bowl, beat the egg yolks and 1 tablespoon of erythritol with an electric whisk until thick and pale. In another bowl, whisk the egg whites at low speed with clean beaters until foamy. Increase the speed, add the remaining erythritol, 1 tablespoon at a time, and whisk until soft peak forms, 3 to 4 minutes. Gently and gradually, fold the egg white mixture into the egg yolk mix.
3. Heat the olive oil in a safe oven non-stick frying pan over low heat. Swirl the pan to spread the oil and pour in the egg mixture; swirl to spread too. Cook for 3 minutes and then, transfer to the oven; bake for 2 to 3 minutes or until golden, puffed, and set.
4. Plate the omelet and spoon the blueberry sauce onto the egg. Use the spoon to spread around. Garnish with lemon zest.
5. Serve immediately with tea or coffee.

Simple Cheese Olives Tomato Salad

Preparation time: 15 minutes

Servings: 4

Nutritional Values (per Serving):

- Calories 67
- Fat 5 g
- Carbohydrates 4 g
- Sugar 1 g
- Protein 2 g
- Cholesterol 4 mg

Ingredients:

- 1 cup kalamata olives, pitted
- 1 cup mozzarella cheese, chopped
- 1 cup cherry tomatoes, halved
- Pepper
- Salt

Directions:

1. Add olives, cheese, and tomatoes in a bowl and toss well.
2. Season with pepper and salt.
3. Serve and enjoy.

Argugula Mushroom Salad

Preparation time: 20 minutes

Servings: 4

Nutritional Values (per Serving):

- Calories 261
- Fat 22 g
- Carbohydrates 14 g
- Sugar 9 g
- Protein 5 g
- Cholesterol 0 mg

Ingredients:

- 10 oz mushrooms, clean and cut the steam
- 10 sun-dried tomatoes, chopped
- 4 cups arugula
- 2 tsp fresh rosemary, chopped
- 2 garlic cloves, minced
- 1 tbsp vinegar
- 6 tbsp olive oil
- 1/2 tsp sea salt

Directions:

1. In a small bowl, combine together olive oil, vinegar, salt, rosemary, and garlic.
2. Add mushroom in a bowl then pour olive oil mixture over mushrooms and set aside for 1 hour.
3. Preheat the oven to 480 F.
4. Place mushrooms on rack and grill in preheated oven for 10 minutes.
5. Place arugula on serving dish then place grilled mushrooms and chopped tomatoes.
6. Serve and enjoy.

Simple Grilled Mushrooms

Preparation time: 25 minutes

Servings: 4

Nutritional Values (Per Serving):

- Calories 295
- Fat 28 g
- Carbohydrates 8 g
- Sugar 3 g
- Protein 5 g
- Cholesterol 0 mg

Ingredients:

- 40 cremini mushrooms
- 1 tsp sea salt
- 1/2 tsp black pepper
- 8 tbsp olive oil

Directions:

1. Preheat the oven to 450 F.
2. Add mushroom and olive oil in a bowl and toss well.
3. Season mushrooms with pepper and salt.

4. Place mushrooms on the rack and grilled in preheated oven for 15 minutes.
5. Serve and enjoy.

Healthy Green Salad with Mayonnaise

Preparation time: 20 minutes

Servings: 2

Nutritional Values (Per Serving):

- Calories 127
- Fat 6 g
- Carbohydrates 14 g
- Sugar 4 g
- Protein 8 g
- Cholesterol 4 mg

Ingredients:

- 2 tbsp mayonnaise
- 2 cups watercress
- 2 cups iceberg lettuce, chopped
- 2 small Bok Choy, chopped
- 2 cups arugula
- Pepper

Directions:

1. Add all ingredients to the bowl and toss well.
2. Serve and enjoy.

Seitan Cauliflower Bowl

Preparation time: 10 minutes

Cooking time: 22 minutes + 1 hour marinating

Servings: 4

Nutritional Values (Per Serving):

- Calories:823
- Total Fat: 75.5g
- Saturated Fat:14 g
- Total Carbs: 8 g
- Dietary Fiber: 2g
- Sugar:2 g
- Protein: 31g
- Sodium: 198mg

Ingredients:

- ¼ cup coconut aminos
- ½ lemon, juiced
- 3 tsp garlic powder
- 1 tbsp swerve sugar
- 1 lb seitan, cut into strips
- 1 cup olive oil
- 6 garlic cloves, minced

- 2 ½ cups cauliflower rice
- 2 tbsp olive oil
- 4 large eggs
- 2 tbsp chopped fresh scallions, for garnishing

Directions:

1. In a medium bowl, mix the coconut aminos, lemon juice, garlic powder, and swerve sugar.
2. Add the seitan, coat well in the mix and marinate for 1 hour.
3. Heat the olive oil in a medium wok and fry the seitan on both sides until brown and cooked through, 10 minutes. Transfer the seitan to a plate and set aside for serving.
4. Sauté the garlic in the wok until fragrant, 30 seconds. Stir in the cauliflower rice until softened, 5 minutes and season with salt and black pepper. Spoon the food into 4 serving bowls and set aside.
5. Wipe the wok clean with a paper towel and heat in 1 tablespoon of olive oil.
6. Crack in two eggs and fry sunshine-style, 1 minute. Place an egg on each cauliflower rice bowl and fry the remaining eggs with the remaining olive oil. Plate also.
7. Divide the seitan on the food, garnish with some scallions, and serve immediately.

Cheesy Mushroom in Omelet

Preparation time: 15 minutes

Cooking time: 20 minutes

Serving: 2

Nutritional Values (Per Serving):

Calories: 199

Total Fat: 15.7g

Saturated Fat:5.1 g

Total Carbs: 4 g

Dietary Fiber: 1g

Sugar: 2g

Protein: 11g

Sodium: 201mg

Ingredients:

- 4 large eggs
- 2 tbsp almond milk
- 2 tbsp olive oil
- 1 medium yellow onion, sliced

- ½ medium green bell pepper, deseeded and sliced
- ¼ lb cremini mushrooms, sliced
- Salt and black pepper to taste
- 2 oz provolone cheese, very thinly sliced

Directions:

1. Beat the eggs with the almond milk in a medium bowl.
2. Heat half of the olive oil in a medium skillet and pour a quarter of the eggs. Fry until cooked on one side, carefully flip with a spatula, and cook until well-done. Slide onto a plate and make three more eggs. Place on different plates when ready.
3. Heat the remaining olive oil in the same skillet and sauté the onion and bell pepper until softened, 5 minutes. Transfer to a plate and set aside.
4. Season the mushrooms with salt and black pepper, add to the skillet, and cook until softened, 5 minutes. Return the onion and pepper to the pan and cook for 1 minute to keep warm. Turn the heat off.
5. Layer the provolone cheese evenly in the omelet and top with the hot mushroom mixture.
6. Roll the eggs and place back in the skillet over low heat to melt the cheese.
7. Transfer to serving plates and serve immediately.

Cajun Tofu in Mushrooms

Preparation time: 10 minutes

Cooking time: 43 minutes

Serving: 4

Nutritional Values (Per Serving):

- Calories: 400
- Total Fat: 29.1g
- Saturated Fat: 8.1g
- Total Carbs: 10 g
- Dietary Fiber:3 g
- Sugar: 2g
- Protein:29 g
- Sodium: 414 mg

Ingredients:

- 2 tbsp olive oil
- ½ celery stalk, chopped
- 1 small red onion, finely chopped
- 1 lb tofu, pressed and crumbled
- Salt and black pepper to taste
- 2 tbsp mayonnaise
- 1 tsp Cajun seasoning

- ½ tsp garlic powder
- ½ cup shredded Gouda cheese
- 2 large eggs
- 4 large caps Portobello mushrooms
- 1 tbsp almond meal
- 2 tbsp shredded Parmesan cheese
- 1 tbsp chopped fresh parsley

Directions:

1. Preheat the oven to 350 F and lightly grease a baking sheet with cooking spray. Set aside.
2. Heat half of the olive oil in a medium skillet over medium heat and sauté the celery, red onion until softened, 3 minutes. Transfer to a medium mixing bowl.
3. Add the remaining olive oil to the skillet, season the tofu with salt, black pepper, and cook until brown, 10 minutes. Turn the heat off and transfer to the same bowl.
4. Pour in the mayonnaise, Cajun seasoning, garlic powder, Gouda cheese, and crack in the eggs. Mix well.
5. Arrange the mushrooms on the baking sheet and fill with the tofu mix.
6. In a small bowl, mix the almond meal, Parmesan cheese, and sprinkle on top of the mushroom filling. Cover with foil and bake in the oven until the cheese melts, 30 minutes.

7. Remove the stuffed mushrooms, take off the foil, and garnish with the parsley.

8. Serve immediately.

Braised Seitan with Kelp Noodles

Preparation time: 10 minutes

Cooking time: 2 hours 2 minutes

Serving: 4

Nutritional Values (Per Serving):

- Calories: 311
- Total Fat: 18g
- Saturated Fat: 6.3g
- Total Carbs: 3 g
- Dietary Fiber:0 g
- Sugar:2 g
- Protein:34 g
- Sodium:136 mg

Ingredients:

- 1 tbsp olive oil
- 2 pieces star anise
- 1 cinnamon stick
- 1 garlic clove, minced

- 1-inch ginger, grated
- 1 ½ lb seitan, cut into strips
- 3 tbsp tamarind sauce
- 2 tbsp swerve sugar
- ¼ cup red wine
- ¼ cup water
- 4 cups vegetable broth
- 2 (23.9oz) kelp noodles, thoroughly rinsed

For topping:

- 1 cup steamed napa cabbage
- Scallions, thinly sliced

Directions:

1. Heat the olive oil in a medium pot over medium heat and stir-fry the star anise, cinnamon, garlic, and ginger until fragrant, 5 minutes.
2. Mix in the seitan, season with salt, black pepper, and sear on both sides, 10 minutes.
3. In a small bowl, combine the tamarind sauce, swerve sugar, red wine, and water. Pour the mixture into the pot, close the lid, and bring to a boil. Reduce the heat and simmer for 30 to 45 minutes or until the seitan is tender.

4. Strain the pot's content through a colander into a bowl and pour the braising liquid back into the pot. Discard the cinnamon, star anise and set the seitan aside.
5. Add the vegetable broth to the pot and simmer until hot, 10 minutes.
6. Put the kelp noodles into the broth and cook until softened and separated, 5 to 7 minutes.
7. Spoon the noodles with some broth into serving bowls, top with the seitan strips, and then the cabbage and scallions.

Roasted Artichokes and Sauce

Preparation time: 10 minutes

Cooking time: 30 minutes

Servings: 4

Nutritional Values (Per Serving):

- Calories 190
- Fat 6
- Fiber 8
- Carbs 10
- Protein 9

Ingredients:

- 2 big artichokes, trimmed and halved
- 2 tablespoons avocado oil
- Juice of 1 lime
- 1 teaspoon turmeric powder
- 1 cup coconut cream
- A pinch of salt and black pepper
- ½ teaspoon onion powder
- ¼ teaspoon sweet paprika

- 1 teaspoon cumin, ground

Directions:

1. In a roasting pan, combine the artichokes with the oil, the lime juice and the other ingredients, toss and bake at 390 degrees F for 30 minutes.
2. Divide the artichokes and sauce between plates and serve.

Zucchini Risotto

Preparation time: 10 minutes

Cooking time: 30 minutes

Servings: 4

Nutritional Values (Per Serving):

- Calories 231
- Fat 5
- Fiber 3
- Carbs 9
- Protein 12

Ingredients:

- ½ cup shallots, chopped
- 2 tablespoons olive oil

- 3 garlic cloves, minced
- 2 cups cauliflower rice
- 1 cup zucchinis, cubed
- 2 cups veggie stock
- ½ cup white mushrooms, chopped
- ½ teaspoon coriander, ground
- A pinch of salt and black pepper
- ¼ teaspoon oregano, dried
- 2 tablespoons parsley, chopped

Directions:

1. Heat up a pan with the oil over medium heat, add the shallots, garlic, mushrooms, coriander and oregano, stir and sauté for 10 minutes.
2. Add the cauliflower rice and the other ingredients, toss, cook for 20 minutes more, divide between plates and serve.

Cabbage and Rice

Preparation time: 10 minutes

Cooking time: 30 minutes

Servings: 4

Nutritional Values (Per Serving):

- Calories 200
- Fat 4
- Fiber 1
- Carbs 8
- Protein 5

Ingredients:

- 1 cup green cabbage, shredded
- 1 cup cauliflower rice
- 2 tablespoons olive oil
- 2 tablespoons tomato passata
- 2 spring onions, chopped
- 2 teaspoons balsamic vinegar
- A pinch of salt and black pepper
- 2 teaspoons fennel seeds, crushed
- 1 teaspoon coriander, ground

Directions:

1. Heat up a pan with the oil over medium heat, add the spring onions, fennel and coriander, stir and cook for 5 minutes.
2. Add the cabbage, cauliflower rice and the other ingredients, toss, cook over medium heat for 25 minutes more, divide between plates and serve.

Tomato Risotto

Preparation time: 10 minutes

Cooking time: 30 minutes

Servings: 4

Nutritional Values (Per Serving):

- Calories 200
- Fat 4
- Fiber 3
- Carbs 6
- Protein 8

Ingredients:

- 1 cup shallots, chopped
- 2 cups cauliflower rice
- 3 tablespoons olive oil
- 2 cups veggie stock
- 1 cup tomatoes, crushed
- ¼ cup cilantro, chopped
- ½ teaspoon chili powder
- 1 teaspoon cumin, ground
- 1 teaspoon coriander, ground

Directions:

1. Heat up a pan with the oil over medium heat, add the shallots and sauté for 5 minutes.
2. Add the cauliflower rice, tomatoes and the other ingredients, toss, cook over medium heat for 25 minutes more, divide between plates and serve.

Herbed Risotto

Preparation time: 10 minutes

Cooking time: 25 minutes

Servings: 4

Nutritional Values (Per Serving):

- Calories 182
- Fat 4
- Fiber 2
- Carbs 8
- Protein 10

Ingredients:

- 2 cups cauliflower rice
- 4 scallions, chopped
- 2 tablespoons avocado oil
- 2 cups veggie stock
- Juice of 1 lime
- 1 tablespoon parsley, chopped
- 1 tablespoon cilantro, chopped
- 1 tablespoon basil, chopped
- 1 tablespoon oregano, chopped

- 1 teaspoon sweet paprika
- A pinch of salt and black pepper

Directions:

1. Heat up a pan with the oil over medium heat, add the scallions and sauté for 5 minutes.
2. Add the cauliflower rice, the stock and the other ingredients, toss, cook over medium heat for 20 minutes, divide between plates and serve as a side dish.

Radish and Broccoli

Preparation time: 10 minutes

Cooking time: 30 minutes

Servings: 4

Nutritional Values (Per Serving):

- Calories 261
- Fat 5
- Fiber 4
- Carbs 9
- Protein 12

Ingredients:

- 2 tablespoons olive oil
- 1 pound broccoli florets
- 4 scallions, chopped
- ½ pound radishes, halved
- 4 garlic cloves, minced
- 2 teaspoons cumin, ground
- 2 tablespoons tomato passata
- ½ cup veggie stock
- A pinch of salt and black pepper

Directions:

1. Heat up a pan with the oil over medium heat, add the scallions and sauté for 5 minutes.
2. Add the broccoli, radishes and the other ingredients, toss, cook over medium heat for 25 minutes more, divide between plates and serve.

Air Fried Zucchini & Squash

Preparation time: 10 minutes

Cooking time: 10 minutes

Servings: 2

Nutritional Values (per Serving):

- Calories 112
- Fat 8.4 g
- Carbohydrates 7.5 g
- Sugar 3.1 g
- Protein 4.2 g
- Cholesterol 4 mg

Ingredients:

- 1 zucchini, sliced
- 1 tbsp butter, melted
- 1 yellow squash, sliced
- 2 tbsp parmesan cheese, grated
- 1 tsp garlic powder
- Pepper
- Salt

Directions:

1. Preheat the air fryer to 375 F.
2. Add all ingredients into the bowl and toss well.
3. Add vegetable mixture into the air fryer basket and cook for 10 minutes.
4. Serve and enjoy.

Mustard Greens and Spinach Soup

Preparation time: 10 minutes

Cooking time: 15 minutes

Servings: 6

Nutritional Values (Per Serving):

- Calories – 143
- Fat – 6
- Fiber – 3
- Carbs – 7

- Protein - 7

Ingredients:

- ½ teaspoon fenugreek seeds
- 1 teaspoon cumin seeds
- 1 tablespoon avocado oil
- 1 teaspoon coriander seeds
- 1 cup onion, chopped
- 1 tablespoon garlic, minced
- 1 tablespoon fresh ginger, grated
- ½ teaspoon turmeric
- 5 cups mustard greens, chopped
- 3 cups coconut milk
- 1 tablespoon jalapeño, chopped
- 5 cups spinach, torn
- Salt and ground black pepper, to taste
- 2 teaspoons butter
- ½ teaspoon paprika

Directions:

1. Heat up a pot with the oil over medium-high heat, add the coriander, fenugreek, and cumin seeds, stir, and brown them for 2 minutes.

2. Add the onions, stir, and cook for 3 minutes. Add the half of the garlic, jalapeños, ginger, and turmeric, stir, and cook for 3 minutes.
3. Add the mustard greens, and spinach, stir, and sauté everything for 10 minutes.
4. Add the milk, salt, and pepper, and blend the soup using an immersion blender.
5. Heat up a pan with the butter over medium heat, add the garlic, and paprika, stir well, and take off the heat.
6. Heat up the soup over medium heat, ladle into soup bowls, drizzle with butter and sprinkle with paprika all over, and serve.

Roasted Asparagus

Preparation time: 10 minutes

Cooking time: 10 minutes

Servings: 3

Nutritional Values (Per Serving):

- Calories – 130
- Fat – 1
- Fiber – 1
- Carbs – 2
- Protein - 3

Ingredients:

- 1 asparagus bunch, trimmed
- 3 teaspoons avocado oil
- A splash of lemon juice
- Salt and ground black pepper, to taste
- 1 tablespoon fresh oregano, chopped

Directions:

1. Spread the asparagus spears on a lined baking sheet, season with salt, and pepper, drizzle with oil and lemon juice, sprinkle with oregano, and toss to coat well.
2. Place in an oven at 425°F, and bake for 10 minutes.
3. Divide on plates and serve.

Asparagus and Browned Butter

Preparation time: 10 minutes

Cooking time: 15 minutes

Servings: 4

Nutritional Values (Per Serving):

- Calories – 160
- Fat – 7
- Fiber – 2
- Carbs – 6
- Protein - 10

Ingredients:

- 5 ounces butter
- 1 tablespoon avocado oil
- 1½ pounds asparagus, trimmed
- 1½ tablespoons lemon juice
- A pinch of cayenne pepper
- 8 tablespoons sour cream
- Salt and ground black pepper, to taste
- 3 ounces Parmesan cheese, grated
- 4 eggs

Directions:

1. Heat up a pan with 2 ounces butter over medium-high heat, add the eggs, some salt and pepper, stir, and scramble them.
2. Transfer the eggs to a blender, add the Parmesan cheese, sour cream, salt, pepper, and cayenne pepper, and blend everything well.
3. Heat up a pan with the oil over medium-high heat, add the asparagus, salt, and pepper, roast for a few minutes, transfer to a plate, and set aside.
4. Heat up the pan again with the rest of the butter over medium-high heat, stir until brown, take off the heat, add the lemon juice, and stir well.
5. Heat up the butter again, return the asparagus to the pan, toss to coat, heat up well, and divide on plates.
6. Add the blended eggs on top and serve.

Asparagus Frittata

Preparation time: 10 minutes

Cooking time: 15 minutes

Servings: 4

Nutritional Values (Per Serving):

- Calories – 200
- Fat – 12
- Fiber – 2
- Carbs – 5
- Protein - 14

Ingredients:

- ¼ cup onion, chopped
- A drizzle of olive oil
- 1 pound asparagus spears, cut into 1-inch pieces
- Salt and ground black pepper, to taste
- 4 eggs, whisked
- 1 cup cheddar cheese, grated

Directions:

1. Heat up a pan with the oil over medium-high heat, add the onions, stir, and cook for 3 minutes.
2. Add the asparagus, stir, and cook for 6 minutes.
3. Add the eggs, stir, and cook for 3 minutes.
4. Add the salt and pepper, sprinkle with the cheese, place in an oven, and broil for 3 minutes.
5. Divide the frittata on plates and serve.

Creamy Asparagus

Preparation time: 10 minutes

Cooking time: 15 minutes

Servings: 3

Nutritional Values (Per Serving):

- Calories – 256
- Fat – 23
- Fiber – 2
- Carbs – 5
- Protein - 13

Ingredients:

- 10 ounces asparagus spears, cut into medium-sized pieces, and steamed
- Salt and ground black pepper, to taste
- 2 tablespoons Parmesan cheese, grated
- ⅓ cup Monterey jack cheese, shredded
- 2 tablespoons mustard
- 2 ounces cream cheese
- ⅓ cup heavy cream
- 3 tablespoons bacon, cooked and crumbled

Directions:

1. Heat up a pan with the mustard, heavy cream, and cream cheese over medium heat and stir well.
2. Add the Monterey Jack cheese, and Parmesan cheese, stir, and cook until it melts.
3. Add the half of the bacon, and the asparagus, stir, and cook for 3 minutes.
4. Add the rest of the bacon, plus salt and pepper, stir, cook for 5 minutes, divide on plates, and serve.

Alfalfa Sprouts Salad

Preparation time: 10 minutes

Cooking time: 0 minutes

Servings: 4

Nutritional Values (Per Serving):

- Calories – 100
- Fat – 3
- Fiber – 1
- Carbs – 2
- Protein - 6

Ingredients:

- 1 green apple, cored, and julienned
- 1½ teaspoons dark sesame oil
- 4 cups alfalfa sprouts
- Salt and ground black pepper, to taste
- 1½ teaspoons grape seed oil
- ¼ cup coconut milk yogurt
- 4 nasturtium leaves

Directions:

1. In a salad bowl, mix the sprouts with apple and nasturtium.
2. Add the salt, pepper, sesame oil, grape seed oil, and coconut yogurt, toss to coat, and divide on plates, and serve.

Root Vegetable Soup

Preparation time: 15 Minutes

Cooking time: 15 Minutes

Servings: 4

Ingredients:

- 2 tablespoons olive oil
- 1 onion, diced
- 3 garlic cloves, minced
- 1 carrot, julienned or grated
- 1 rutabaga, julienned or grated
- 1 parsnip, julienned or grated
- 1 red potato, julienned or grated
- 5 cups vegetable stock
- 2 teaspoons dried thyme sea salt
- freshly ground black pepper

Directions:

1. In a large soup pot, heat the olive oil over medium-high heat until it shimmers.

2. Add the onion and cook until it softens, about 5 minutes. Add the garlic and cook until it is fragrant, about 30 seconds. Add the carrot, rutabaga, parsnip, potato, vegetable stock, and thyme. Cover and boil until vegetables soften, about 10 minutes.

3. Remove from the heat. Using a food processor or blender, purée the soup in batches. Season with salt and pepper. Serve immediately.

Minestrone

Preparation time: 15 Minutes

Cooking time: 15 Minutes

Servings: 4

Ingredients:

- 2 tablespoons olive oil
- ½ onion, diced
- 1 carrot, peeled and diced
- 1 stalk celery, diced
- 4 garlic cloves, minced
- 5 cups vegetable stock
- 1 zucchini, diced
- one 15-ounce can kidney beans, drained and rinsed

- one 15-ounce can chopped tomatoes with liquid, or 2 fresh tomatoes, peeled and chopped
- 2 teaspoons italian seasoning
- sea salt
- freshly ground pepper

Directions:

1. In a large soup pot, heat the olive oil over medium-high heat until it shimmers.
2. Add the onion, carrot, and celery and cook until vegetables soften, about 5 minutes. Add the garlic and cook until it is fragrant, about 30 seconds. Add the vegetable stock, zucchini, kidney beans, tomatoes, and Italian seasoning. Simmer the soup until the vegetables are soft, about 10 minutes. Season with salt and pepper and serve immediately.

Black Bean and Corn Soup

Preparation time: 5 Minutes

Cooking time: 50 Minutes

Servings: 4

Ingredients:

- 2 tablespoons olive oil
- 1 medium red onion, chopped
- 1 medium red or yellow bell pepper, chopped
- 1 medium carrot, minced
- 4 garlic cloves, minced
- 1 teaspoon ground cumin
- 1 teaspoon dried oregano
- 1 (14.5-ounce) can diced tomatoes, drained
- 4 ½ cups cooked or 3 (15.5-ounce) cans black beans, rinsed and drained
- 6 cups vegetable broth (homemade, store-bought, or water)
- 2 cups fresh, frozen, or canned corn kernels
- 1 teaspoon fresh lemon juice
- Salt and freshly ground black pepper
- Tabasco sauce, to serve

Directions:

1. In a large soup pot, heat the oil over medium heat. Add the onion, bell pepper, carrot, and garlic, cover, and cook until soft, about 10 minutes. Uncover and stir in the cumin and oregano, tomatoes, beans, and broth. Bring to a boil, then reduce heat to low and simmer, uncovered, for 30 minutes, stirring occasionally.

2. Puree about one-third of the soup in the pot with an immersion blender, or in a blender or food processor, then return to the pot. Add the corn, and simmer uncovered, for 10 minutes to heat through and blend flavors.

3. Just before serving, stir in the lemon juice and season with salt and pepper to taste. Ladle into bowls and serve with hot sauce on the side.

Creamy Tofu with Green Beans and Keto Fettuccine

Preparation time: 40 minutes + overtime chilling time
Serving size: 4

Nutritional Values (Per Serving):

- Calories:721
- Total Fat:76.8g
- Saturated Fat:21.2g
- Total Carbs:2g
- Dietary Fiber:0g
- Sugar:0g
- Protein:9g
- Sodium:309mg

Ingredients:

For the keto fettuccine:

- 1 cup shredded mozzarella cheese
- 1 egg yolk

For the creamy tofu and green beans:

- 1 tbsp olive oil
- 4 tofu, cut into thin strips
- Salt and black pepper to taste
- ½ cup green beans, chopped
- 1 lemon, zested and juiced
- ¼ cup vegetable broth
- 1 cup plain yogurt
- 6 basil leaves, chopped
- 1 cup shaved parmesan cheese for topping

Directions:

For the keto fettucine:

1. Pour the cheese into a medium safe-microwave bowl and melt in the microwave for 35 minutes or until melted.
2. Take out the bowl and allow cooling for 1 minute only to warm the cheese but not cool completely. Mix in the egg yolk until well-combined.
3. Lay a parchment paper on a flat surface, pour the cheese mixture on top and cover with another parchment paper. Using a rolling pin, flatten the dough into 1/8-inch thickness.

4. Take off the parchment paper and cut the dough into thick fettuccine strands. Place in a bowl and refrigerate overnight.

5. When ready to cook, bring 2 cups of water to a boil in medium saucepan and add the keto fettuccine. Cook for 40 seconds to 1 minute and then drain through a colander. Run cold water over the pasta and set aside to cool.

For the creamy tofu and green beans:

6. Heat the olive oil in a large skillet, season the tofu with salt, black pepper, and cook in the oil until brown on the outside and slightly cooked through, 10 minutes.

7. Mix in the green beans and cook until softened, 5 minutes.

8. Stir in the lemon zest, lemon juice, and vegetable broth. Cook for 5 more minutes or until the liquid reduces by a quarter.

9. Add the plain yogurt and mix well. Pour in the keto fettuccine and basil, fold in well and cook for 1 minute. Adjust the taste with salt and black pepper as desired.

10. Dish the food onto serving plates, top with the parmesan cheese and serve warm.

Sunshine Fiesta Salad

Preparation time: 15 Minutes

Cooking time: 0 Minutes

Servings: 4

Ingredients:

For the Vinaigrette

- Juice of 2 limes
- 1 tablespoon olive oil
- 1 tablespoon maple syrup or agave
- ¼ teaspoon sea salt

For the Salad

- 2 cups cooked quinoa
- 1 tablespoon Taco Seasoning or store-bought taco seasoning
- 2 heads romaine lettuce, roughly chopped
- 1 (15-ounce) can black beans, rinsed and drained
- 1 cup cherry tomatoes, halved
- 1 cup frozen (and thawed) or fresh corn kernels
- 1 avocado, peeled, pitted, and diced
- 4 scallions, thinly sliced

- 12 tortilla chips, crushed

Directions:

For the vinaigrette:

1. In a small bowl, whisk together all the vinaigrette ingredients.

For the salad:

2. In a medium bowl, mix together the quinoa and taco seasoning. In a large bowl, toss the romaine with the vinaigrette. Divide among 4 bowls. Top each bowl with equal amounts quinoa, beans, tomatoes, corn, avocado, scallions, and crushed tortillas chips.

French-Style Potato Salad

Preparation time: 5 Minutes

Cooking time: 30 Minutes

Servings: 4 To 6

Ingredients:

- 1½ pounds small white potatoes, unpeeled
- 2 tablespoons minced fresh parsley
- 1 tablespoon minced fresh chives
- 1 teaspoon minced fresh tarragon or ½ teaspoon dried
- ⅓ cup olive oil
- 2 tablespoons white wine or tarragon vinegar

- ⅛ teaspoon freshly ground black pepper

Directions:

1. In a large pot of boiling salted water, cook the potatoes until tender but still firm, about 30 minutes. Drain and cut into ¼-inch slices. Transfer to a large bowl and add the parsley, chives, and tarragon. Set aside.
2. In a small bowl, combine the oil, vinegar, pepper. Pour the dressing onto the potato mixture and toss gently to combine.
3. Taste, adjusting seasonings if necessary. Chill for 1 to 2 hours before serving.

Roasted Carrot Salad

Preparation time: 10 Minutes

Cooking time: 30 Minutes

Servings: 3

Ingredients:

- 4 carrots, peeled and sliced
- 1 to 2 teaspoons olive oil or coconut oil
- ½ teaspoon ground cinnamon or pumpkin pie spice
- Salt
- 1 (15-ounce) can cannellini beans or navy beans, drained and rinsed
- 3 cups chopped hearty greens, such as spinach, kale, chard, or collards
- ⅓ cup dried cranberries or pomegranate seeds
- ⅓ cup slivered almonds or Cinnamon-Lime Sunflower Seeds
- ¼ cup Raspberry Vinaigrette or Cilantro-Lime Dressing, or 2 tablespoons freshly squeezed orange or lemon juice whisked with 2 tablespoons olive oil and a pinch of salt

Directions:

1. Preheat the oven or toaster oven to 400°F.

2. In a medium bowl, toss the carrots with the olive oil and cinnamon and season to taste with salt. Transfer to a small tray, and roast for 15 minutes or until browned around the edges. Toss the carrots, add the beans, and roast for 15 minutes more. Let cool while you prep the salad. Divide the greens among three plates or containers, top with the cranberries and almonds, and add the roasted carrots and beans.

3. Drizzle with the dressing of your choice. Store leftovers in an airtight container in the refrigerator for up to 1 week.

Roasted Potato Salad with Chickpeas and Tomatoes

Preparation time: 5 Minutes

Cooking time: 20 Minutes

Servings: 4 To 6

Ingredients:

- 1½ pounds Yukon Gold potatoes, cut into ½-inch dice
- 1 medium shallot, halved lengthwise and cut into ¼-inch slices
- ¼ cup olive oil
- Salt and freshly ground black pepper
- 3 tablespoons white wine vinegar
- 1½ cups cooked or 1 (15.5-ounce) can chickpeas, drained and rinsed
- ⅓ cup chopped drained oil-packed sun-dried tomatoes
- ¼ cup green olives, pitted and halved
- ¼ cup chopped fresh parsley

Directions:

1. Preheat the oven to 425°F. In a large bowl, combine the potatoes, shallot, and 1 tablespoon of the oil. Season with

salt and pepper to taste and toss to coat. Transfer the potatoes and shallot to a baking sheet and roast, turning once, until tender and golden brown, about 20 minutes. Transfer to a large bowl and set aside to cool.

2. In a small bowl, combine the remaining 3 tablespoons oil with the vinegar and pepper to taste. Add the chickpeas, tomatoes, olives, and parsley to the cooked potatoes and shallots. Drizzle with the dressing and toss gently to combine. Taste, adjusting seasonings if necessary. Serve warm or at room temperature.

Carrot Cake Bites

Preparation time: 15 minutes

Cooking time: 0 minute

Servings: 15

Nutritional Values (Per Serving):

- Calories: 87 Cal
- Fat: 5 g
- Carbs: 9.2 g
- Protein: 1.8 g
- Fiber: 1.6 g

Ingredients:

- 2 cups oats, old-fashioned
- ½ cup grated carrot
- 2 cups coconut flakes, unsweetened
- 1/2 teaspoon salt
- 1 teaspoon cinnamon
- 1/2 cup maple syrup
- 1/2 teaspoon vanilla extract, unsweetened
- 1/2 cup almond butter

- 2 tablespoons white chocolate chips

Directions:

1. Place oats in a food processor, add coconut and pulse until ground.
2. Then add remaining ingredients except for chocolate chips and pulse for 3 minutes until a sticky dough comes together.
3. Add chocolate chips, pulse for 1 minute until just mixed, and then shape the mixture into fifteen small balls.
4. Refrigerate the balls for 30 minutes and then serve.

Cinnamon Bun Balls

Preparation time: 15 minutes

Cooking time: 0 minute

Servings: 10

Nutritional Values (Per Serving):

- Calories:62 Cal
- Fat: 4.5
- Carbs: 5.8 g
- Protein: 1.2 g
- Fiber: 2 g

Ingredients:

- 5 medjool dates, pitted
- 1/2 cup whole walnuts
- 1 tablespoon chopped walnuts
- 3 tablespoons ground cinnamon
- 1 teaspoon ground cardamom

Directions:

1. Place all the ingredients in a food processor, except for 1 tablespoon walnuts, and then process until smooth.
2. Shape the mixture into ten balls, then roll them into chopped walnuts and serve.

Kale Hummus

Preparation time: 5 minutes

Cooking time: 0 minute

Servings: 4

Nutritional Values (Per Serving):

- Calories: 173 Cal
- Fat: 10 g
- Carbs: 14 g
- Protein: 6 g
- Fiber: 5 g

Ingredients:

- 2 cups cooked chickpeas
- 5 cloves of garlic, peeled
- 4 cups kale, torn into pieces
- 1 teaspoon of sea salt
- 1/3 cup lemon juice
- 1/4 cup olive oil
- 1/4 cup tahini

Directions:

1. Place all the ingredients in a bowl and pulse for 2 minutes until smooth.
2. Tip the hummus in a bowl, drizzle with oil, and then serve.

Zesty Orange-Cranberry Energy Bites

Preparation time: 10 minutes

Chill Time: 15 minutes

Serves: 12 bites

Nutrition (1 bite):

- Calories: 109
- Total fat: 7g
- Carbs: 11g
- Fiber: 3g
- Protein: 3g

Ingredients:

- 2 tablespoons almond butter, or cashew or sunflower seed butter
- 2 tablespoons maple syrup, or brown rice syrup
- ¾ cup cooked quinoa
- ¼ cup sesame seeds, toasted
- 1 tablespoon chia seeds
- ½ teaspoon almond extract, or vanilla extract
- Zest of 1 orange

- 1 tablespoon dried cranberries
- ¼ cup ground almonds

Directions:

1. In a medium bowl, mix together the nut or seed butter and syrup until smooth and creamy. Stir in the rest of the ingredients, and mix to make sure the consistency is holding together in a ball. Form the mix into 12 balls.
2. Place them on a baking sheet lined with parchment or waxed paper and put in the fridge to set for about 15 minutes.
3. If your balls aren't holding together, it's likely because of the moisture content of your cooked quinoa.
4. Add more nut or seed butter mixed with syrup until it all sticks together.

Chocolate Melt Chaffles

Preparation time: 15 minutes

Cooking time: 36 minutes

Servings: 4

Nutritional Values (Per Serving):

- Calories 172
- Fats 13.57g
- Carbs 6.65g
- Net Carbs 3.65g
- Protein 5.76g

Ingredients:

For the chaffles:

- 2 eggs, beaten
- ¼ cup finely grated Gruyere cheese
- 2 tbsp heavy cream
- 1 tbsp coconut flour
- 2 tbsp cream cheese, softened
- 3 tbsp unsweetened cocoa powder
- 2 tsp vanilla extract
- A pinch of salt

For the chocolate sauce:

- 1/3 cup + 1 tbsp heavy cream
- 1 ½ oz unsweetened baking chocolate, chopped
- 1 ½ tsp sugar-free maple syrup
- 1 ½ tsp vanilla extract

Directions:

For the chaffles:

1. Preheat the cast iron pan.
2. In a medium bowl, mix all the ingredients for the chaffles.
3. Open the iron and add a quarter of the mixture. Close and cook until crispy, 7 minutes.
4. Transfer the chaffle to a plate and make 3 more with the remaining batter.

For the chocolate sauce:

5. Pour the heavy cream into saucepan and simmer over low heat, 3 minutes.
6. Turn the heat off and add the chocolate. Allow melting for a few minutes and stir until fully melted, 5 minutes.
7. Mix in the maple syrup and vanilla extract.
8. Assemble the chaffles in layers with the chocolate sauce sandwiched between each layer.
9. Slice and serve immediately.

Chaffles with Keto Ice Cream

Preparation time: 10 minutes

Cooking time: 14 minutes

Servings: 2

Nutritional Values (Per Serving):

- Calories 89
- Fats 6.48g
- Carbs 1.67g
- Net Carbs 1.37g
- Protein 5.91g

Ingredients:

- 1 egg, beaten
- ½ cup finely grated mozzarella cheese
- ¼ cup almond flour
- 2 tbsp swerve confectioner's sugar

- 1/8 tsp xanthan gum
- Low-carb ice cream (flavor of your choice) for serving

Directions:

1. Preheat the cast iron pan.
2. In a medium bowl, mix all the ingredients except the ice cream.
3. Open the iron and add half of the mixture. Close and cook until crispy, 7 minutes.
4. Transfer the chaffle to a plate and make second one with the remaining batter.
5. On each chaffle, add a scoop of low carb ice cream, fold into half-moons and enjoy.

Cocoa Berries Mousse

Preparation time: 10 minutes

Cooking time: 0 minutes

Servings: 2

Nutritional Values (Per Serving):

- Calories 200
- Fat 8
- Fiber 3.4
- Carbs 7.6
- Protein 4.3

Ingredients:

- 1 tablespoon cocoa powder
- 1 cup blackberries
- 1 cup blueberries
- ¾ cup coconut cream
- 1 tablespoon stevia

Directions:

1. In a blender, combine the berries with the cocoa and the other ingredients, pulse well, divide into bowls and keep in the fridge for 2 hours before serving.

Nutmeg Pudding

Preparation time: 10 minutes

Cooking time: 20 minutes

Servings: 6

Nutritional Values (Per Serving):

- Calories 220
- Fat 6.6
- Fiber 3.4
- Carbs 12.4
- Protein 3.4

Ingredients:

- 2 tablespoons stevia
- 1 teaspoon nutmeg, ground
- 1 cup cauliflower rice
- 2 tablespoons flaxseed mixed with 3 tablespoons water
- 2 cups almond milk
- ¼ teaspoon nutmeg, grated

Directions:

1. In a pan, combine the cauliflower rice with the flaxseed mix and the other ingredients, whisk, cook over medium heat for 20 minutes, divide into bowls and serve cold.

Lime Cherries and Rice Pudding

Preparation time: 10 minutes

Cooking time: 25 minutes

Servings: 4

Nutritional Values (Per Serving):

- Calories 199
- Fat 5.4
- Fiber 3.4
- Carbs 11.5
- Protein 5.6

Ingredients:

- ¾ cup stevia
- 2 cups coconut milk
- 3 tablespoons flaxseed mixed with 4 tablespoons water
- Juice of 2 limes
- Zest of 1 lime, grated
- 1 cup cherries, pitted and halved
- 1 cup cauliflower rice

Directions:

1. In a pan, combine the milk with the stevia and bring to a simmer over medium heat.
2. Add the cauliflower rice and the other ingredients, stir, cook for 25 minutes more, divide into cups and serve cold.

Chocolate Pudding

Preparation time: 10 minutes

Cooking time: 20 minutes

Servings: 4

Nutritional Values (Per Serving):

- Calories 134
- Fat 14.1
- Fiber 0.8
- Carbs 3.1
- Protein 0.9

Ingredients:

- 2 tablespoons cocoa powder
- 2 tablespoons coconut oil, melted
- 2/3 cup coconut cream
- 2 tablespoons stevia
- ¼ teaspoon almond extract

Directions:

1. In a pan, combine the cocoa powder with the coconut milk and the other ingredients, whisk, bring to a simmer ad cook over medium heat for 20 minutes.
2. Divide into cups and serve cold.

Coffee and Rhubarb Cream

Preparation time: 10 minutes

Cooking time: 20 minutes

Servings: 4

Nutritional Values (Per Serving):

- Calories 300
- Fat 30.8
- Fiber 0
- Carbs 3
- Protein 4

Ingredients:

- ¼ cup brewed coffee
- 2 tablespoons stevia
- 2 cups coconut cream
- 1 teaspoon vanilla extract
- 2 tablespoons coconut oil, melted
- 1 cup rhubarb, chopped
- 2 tablespoons flaxseed mixed with 3 tablespoons water

Directions:

1. In a bowl, mix the coffee with stevia, cream and the other ingredients, whisk well and divide into 4 ramekins.
2. Introduce the ramekins in the oven at 350 degrees F, bake for 20 minutes and serve warm.

Avocado and Grapes Shake Bowls

Preparation time: 5 minutes

Cooking time: 0 minutes

Servings: 4

Nutritional Values (Per Serving):

- Calories 328
- Fat 30.4
- Fiber 8
- Carbs 16.1
- Protein 3.1

Ingredients:

- 2 avocados, peeled, pitted and chopped
- 1 cup grapes, halved
- Juice of 1 lime
- ¾ cup almond milk
- ½ teaspoon vanilla extract

Directions:

1. In a blender, combine the avocados with the grapes and the other ingredients, pulse well, divide into bowls and serve cold.

Chia Squares

Preparation time: 30 minutes

Cooking time: 0 minutes

Servings: 4

Nutritional Values (Per Serving):

- Calories 349
- Fat 32.5
- Fiber 12
- Carbs 15.8
- Protein 4.1

Ingredients:

- 1 cup avocado oil
- 2 avocados, peeled, pitted and mashed
- ¼ cup coconut cream
- 1 tablespoon stevia
- ¼ cup lime juice
- 1 tablespoon chia seeds
- A pinch of lemon zest, grated

Directions:

1. In your food processor, combine the avocados with the oil, the cream and the other ingredients, pulse well and spread on the bottom of a pan.
2. Introduce in the fridge for 30 minutes, slice into squares and serve.

Blackberry Pie

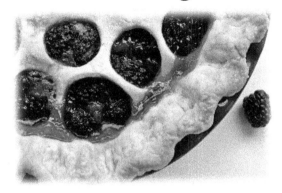

Preparation time: 10 minutes

Cooking time: 35 minutes

Servings: 6

Nutritional Values (Per Serving):

- Calories 231
- Fat 5.5
- Fiber 24
- Carbs 42.3
- Protein 7.2

Ingredients:

- ¾ cup stevia cups blackberries

- ¼ teaspoon baking soda
- 1 tablespoon lime juice
- 1 cup coconut flour
- ½ cup water
- 3 tablespoons avocado oil
- Cooking spray

Directions:

1. In a bowl, combine the blackberries with the stevia, baking soda and the other ingredients, stir well and transfer to a pie pan.
1. Introduce the pan in the oven at 375 degrees F, bake for 35 minutes, slice and serve warm.

Crispy Flaxseed Waffles (ovo)

Preparation time: 15 minutes

Cooking time: 20 minutes

Servings: 8

Nutritions:

- Calories: 204kcal
- Net Carbs: 1.5g
- Fat: 18g
- Protein: 8g
- Fiber: 5.9g
- Sugar: 0.3g

Ingredients:

- 2 cups golden flaxseed (if available, use golden flaxseed meal)
- 1 tbsp. baking powder
- 5 large organic eggs (for vegan waffles, replace with 5 flax eggs)
- ½ cup water (slightly more if necessary)
- ⅓ cup extra virgin olive oil

- 1 tbsp. ground cinnamon
- 1 tbsp. pure vanilla extract
- 6-12 drops stevia sweetener (or more depending on desired sweetness)
- Pinch of salt
- Optional: ¼ cup toasted coconut flakes

Directions:

1. Preheat a waffle maker. If you don't have a waffle maker, heat a medium-sized skillet over medium- high heat for crispy flaxseed pancakes. Grease the waffle maker or skillet with a pinch of olive oil.

2. Take a medium-sized bowl and combine the flaxseed (or flaxseed meal) with the baking powder, eggs, water, remaining olive oil, and a pinch of salt. Incorporate all ingredients by using a whisk and allow the mixture to sit for 5 minutes.

3. Transfer the mixture to a blender or food processor and blend until foamy.

4. Pour the mixture back into the bowl and allow it to sit for another 3 minutes.

5. Add the remaining dry ingredients except the optional toasted coconut flakes—and incorporate everything by using a whisk.

6. Scoop ¼ of the mixture into the waffle maker or skillet. Cook until a firm waffle or pancake has formed. When using a skillet, carefully flip the pancake.
7. Repeat this process for the 3 remaining parts of the batter.
8. Serve the waffles (or pancakes) with the optional toasted coconut flakes and enjoy!
9. Alternatively, store the waffles in an airtight container, keep them in the fridge, and consume within 3 days. Store for a maximum of 30 days in the freezer and thaw at room temperature.

Chocolate-Vanilla Almond Milk (vegan)

Preparation time: 5 minutes

Cooking time: 0 minute

Servings: 1

Nutritions:

- Calories: 422kcal
- Net Carbs: 1.3g
- Fat: 34.8g
- Protein: 25.5g
- Fiber: 2.7g
- Sugar: 0.8g

Ingredients:

- 2 tbsp. coconut oil
- 1½ cups unsweetened almond milk
- ½ vanilla stick (crushed)
- 1 scoop organic soy protein powder (chocolate flavor)
- 4-6 drops stevia sweetener
- Optional: ½ tsp. cinnamon
- Optional: 1-2 ice cubes

Directions:

1. Add all the listed ingredients to a blender—except the
   ice—but including the optional cinnamon if desired.
2. Blend the ingredients for 1 minute; then if desired, add
   the optional ice cubes and blend for another 30 seconds.
3. Transfer the milk to a large cup or shaker, top with some
   additional cinnamon, serve, and enjoy!
4. Alternatively, store the smoothie in an airtight container
   or a mason jar, keep it in the fridge, and consume within
   3 days. Store for a maximum of 30 days in the freezer and
   thaw at room temperature.

Nutty Protein Shake (vegan)

Preparation time: 5 minutes

Cooking time: 0 minute

Servings: 1

Nutritions:

- Calories: 618kcal
- Net Carbs: 4.4g
- Fat: 51.3g
- Protein: 34g
- Fiber: 4.9g
- Sugar: 3g

Ingredients:

- 2 tbsp. coconut oil
- 2 cups unsweetened almond milk
- 2 tbsp. peanut butter
- 1 scoop organic soy protein powder (chocolate flavor)
- 2-4 ice cubes
- 4-6 drops stevia sweetener
- Optional: 1 tsp. vegan creamer
- Optional: 1 tsp. cocoa powder

Directions:

1. Add all the above listed ingredients—except the optional ingredients—to a blender, and blend for 2 minutes.
2. Transfer the shake to a large cup or shaker. If desired, top the shake with the optional vegan creamer and/or cocoa powder.
3. Stir before serving, and enjoy!
4. Alternatively, store the smoothie in an airtight container or a mason jar, keep it in the fridge, and consume within 3 days. Store for a maximum of 30 days in the freezer and thaw at room temperature.

Chia & Coco Shake (vegan)

Preparation time: 5 minutes

Cooking time: 0 minute

Servings: 2

Nutritions:

- Calories: 509kcal
- Net Carbs: 5.4g
- Fat: 44.55g
- Protein: 20.3g
- Fiber: 7.45g
- Sugar: 3.5g

Ingredients:

- 1 tbsp. chia seeds
- 6 tbsp. water
- 1 cup full-fat coconut milk
- 2 tbsp. peanut butter
- 1 tbsp. MCT oil (or coconut oil)
- 1 scoop organic soy protein powder (chocolate flavor)
- Pinch of Himalayan salt
- 2-4 ice cubes or ½ cup of water

Directions:

1. Mix the chia seeds and 6 tablespoons of water in a small bowl; let sit for at least 30 minutes.
2. Transfer the soaked chia seeds and all other listed ingredients to a blender and blend for 2 minutes.
3. Transfer the shake to a large cup or shaker, serve, and enjoy!
4. Alternatively, store the smoothie in an airtight container or a mason jar, keep it in the fridge, and consume within 3 days. Store for a maximum of 30 days in the freezer and thaw at room temperature.

Fat-Rich Protein Espresso (vegan)

Preparation time: 5 minutes

Cooking time: 0 minute

Servings: 1

Nutritions:

- Calories: 441kcal
- Net Carbs: 5.6g
- Fat: 34.8g
- Protein: 25.4g
- Fiber: 6.9g
- Sugar: 2.8g

Ingredients:

- 1 cup espresso (freshly brewed)
- 2 tbsp. coconut butter (or alternatively, use coconut oil)
- 1 scoop organic soy protein (chocolate flavor)
- ½ vanilla stick
- 4 ice cubes or ½ cup boiled water
- Optional: 1 tbsp. cacao powder
- Optional: ½ tsp. cinnamon
- 2 tbsp. coconut cream

Directions:

1. Make sure to use fresh, hot espresso.
2. Add all the listed ingredients to a heat-safe blender, including the ice or boiled water and optional ingredients (if desired). Use ice to make iced espresso, or hot water for a warm treat.
3. Blend the ingredients for 1 minute and transfer to a large coffee cup.
4. Top the coffee with the coconut cream, stir, serve and enjoy!
5. Alternatively, store the smoothie in an airtight container or a mason jar, keep it in the fridge, and consume within 3 days. Store for a maximum of 30 days in the freezer and thaw at room temperature.

Lightning Source UK Ltd.
Milton Keynes UK
UKHW020652120521
383581UK00005B/40